# UNDER YOUR INFLUENCE

*poems by*

# Ben Westlie

*Finishing Line Press*
Georgetown, Kentucky

# UNDER YOUR INFLUENCE

Copyright © 2017 by Ben Westliie
ISBN 978-1-63534-085-3 First Edition
All rights reserved under International and Pan-American Copyright Conventions. No part of this book may be reproduced in any manner whatsoever without written permission from the publisher, except in the case of brief quotations embodied in critical articles and reviews.

## ACKNOWLEDGMENTS

I would like to thank my Mom for being my best friend, her undefinable love, and for being my shield that helped deflect the loneliness of some pretty sad arrows.

My friends who allow me to show up everyday in their lives and let me be myself even when I'm just a little crazy, overwhelming, and at times unbearable and for the laughter, and the unexpected hugs that remind me that with some people I'm wanted.

To my readers I cant even fathom I have enough people who enjoy my poems to write this sentence, but I hope you find something in here that moves you, intrigues you, or even mirrors a part of yourself that may shimmer a small light on a person you were or may be becoming.

Thank you to all of my mentors and their wisdom and insight, all the writers and their words I'm so in love with, to all the musicians and their music and lyrics for choosing to be artists and for working so hard at that dream so I could be inspired and be reminded to continue to do just the same.

Leah Maines you are a goddess and my biggest fan and advocate and I'm grateful for your kindness and love and I'm honored to be with Finishing Line Press.

Christen Kincaid you've been there to see and overlook every word I've ever published and to be that close to my heart as you can ever get I'm so glad you're there and stayed.

Finally, to my therapist who helped me realize that I have Dependant Personalty Disorder which is perfectly fine and this entire chapbook pays homage to because I will always be more myself under the influence of others.

Publisher: Leah Maines
Editor: Christen Kincaid
Author Photo: Sarah Dowden
Cover Design: Elizabeth Maines

Printed in the USA on acid-free paper.
Order online: www.finishinglinepress.com
        also available on amazon.com

Author inquiries and mail orders:
Finishing Line Press
P. O. Box 1626
Georgetown, Kentucky 40324
U. S. A.

# Table of Contents

Conversing with Ghosts ............................................................. 1
Untrue ........................................................................................ 3
Downtown ................................................................................. 4
Dark ........................................................................................... 5
Reckless ..................................................................................... 6
One Summer Day ..................................................................... 7
Silver Beetle ............................................................................. 9
Truth Chamber ...................................................................... 10
Glove Box ................................................................................ 11
Dial .......................................................................................... 12
Demon ..................................................................................... 13
Driver's Seat ........................................................................... 14
Doll .......................................................................................... 15
Weapon ................................................................................... 16
Crystal ..................................................................................... 17
Omen ....................................................................................... 18
Banner ..................................................................................... 19

*I tell my love to wreck it all.*
*Cut out all the ropes and let me fall.*
*My, my, my, my, my, my, my,*
*right in the moment this order's tall.*

*Bon Iver*

## Conversing with Ghosts

*It's happening all over again.*
                        Your therapist tells you.
Her sentence should not have ended there.
           So open
                      with no reasons to assure your stability.
Obsessive,
              like learning lessons
                    repeat, repeat
attempting to clarify
                  an astray part of yourself.
*I can't control this.*
                      You knew this was your next sentence
            your only defense, your split out of here
like packing
                  for these new wild tomorrows
            you're so terrified
                  to wake up in.
You want to take
                  the conversation
            somewhere
you've never been.
                  These expensive minutes
where all you expect is a fresh outcome.
                  Theories written by scholars, intellectuals
those who would never be
                  in this chair.
*You're in the same place.*
                  She declares.
                        This is not allowed
this conversing with ghosts.
                  *Where can I hide?*      You ask.
                                How can you live outside
            yourself?           You think.

Every room in your life
                                        has these eerie echoes
                  of your sad faint voices
you can never get back to,
                            to listen to, to finish your thoughts.
*You know exactly what's wrong with you.* She decides.
                    You hear this enthusiasm
                            like a soothing vibrato
and the office door closes.
                    You walk into the rest
                          of the day
as if you're renewed, somehow morphed,
      someone who had never come undone, a settled worry.

**Untrue**

You want to remember the day
you started telling the truth.
The moment the lies left you.
Humans make so many choices in just a day-
it's really no mystery, you wake up older.
You always thought that when you fell
asleep your last thought would be your first,
though he's nowhere in your mornings.

## Downtown

The moon, full as a glass of milk,
      how you desired to drink it just to see if something would rise
           within you.
You could be anywhere and you're here trying to live
      out who you think you are.
           You're trying to get lost like you were told to do
by so many people.
      Direction is a charade of a game where no one guesses right.
In the night
      to the bars, the silver beetle's windows are down,
           singing out and inhaling the icy air of midnight hours.
      You are
           tipsy like looking through frosted windows,
this is about seeing your future faces.
      Coming out
           you sing,
what the radio has to offer, you
      dance in the sliver beetle
           like music video vixens.
The silver beetle slides over the white line, recklessly.
      Soon you'll be
downtown where the lights are a burning invite.
      Aglow is the milky moon
           and anxious voices of strangers summoned up into the
blacken sky.

# Dark

You want to learn a few more things.
You want the answers to tell your friends for the moments you seem crazy.
As if your mind was that of a chameleon's skin changing by what it touches.
How lonely it is to be unknown.
Sometimes you think of pictures of people who run away wondering
if they want to stay lost and hidden from becoming irrelevant.
Do we have to have something break within us to fit in our days?
That lesson must have been a day in your childhood where you were absent.
You know we are all shuffling somewhere and we think home is somewhere outside of us. If you could you would freeze your heart and somehow shatter it
and hide every slender shard then going would be like finding and being is somewhere you're getting to.
Today you're a case no one has filed and nobody will re-open.
You're frightened of happiness because that means being in love and having someone love you back. That must have been the lecture you couldn't keep your eyes open for-the lecture you didn't get enough sleep to listen to.
No one can call you crazy unless you committed yourself to the title.
Sometimes when you're alone and talking to yourself it sounds as if there's a choir of loving voices harmonizing your heart into lyric.
You close the blinds and miss out on the day surrounding your house and watch the glow of the room fade and you're not afraid to learn from the hours in your dark.

**Reckless**

You know there are parties happening
you weren't invited to.
You lean closer to your window in hopes to hear laughter
to hear music, to hear conversations
you'll never be a part of.

You step away from the window
and into a reckless thought
you repeat eight times pretty words you were told
when you were part of the social supernova.
You have to prove it's acceptable to speak
to yourself when no one else is there to respond.

You prepare yourself for the unraveling.
You prepare yourself that the rest of your life may be
your ears next to windows and the making up of moments.

You should go to bed
and remember the moon will always want to be near you.
You should count the stars, add them up out loud until you reach
a celestial number that restores your belief in believing.

## One Summer Day

You walked in on him
two bottles hidden in his closet,

It was so serene in this room,
there was light coming through the curtains,
you're not sure what you said to him.

The bottles were just in his fists
they took in the speckled light
the liquid shimmered, to take a sip
would be to ignite.

You slowly paced closer to him
less fearful of his little demon.
What were you doing there?
How did you know his need?
Suddenly, you looked passed him
A bottle of aspirin on his desk.

You thought you saw a ghost,
it was of a haunting state of mind.
We were so much better than happy
on those summer days.

Your eyes called upon clarity
and found his,
they were wet like your sweaty sunny skin.

You were terrified
like seeing a vision of yourself
living without him.

Sometimes things happen to people
and they're not
equipped to deal with them.

Enduring, that's the part of being human
that makes the most sense.

You stayed in that room
the entire day
his head on your chest, your comforting fingers in his hair.

You remember how you kept looking
over his shoulder
as if you could see a prayer of togetherness was sent, received, answered,
drifting into the room.

**Silver Beetle**

You would take the silver beetle
        drive it for days
                until you caught up with what you
had for him.
        You were the only human in his life
                without the need for closeness.
You would make sure the windows were down
        at all times, so the inside
                wouldn't miss the outside.
        The silver beetle took you everywhere.
So much of your lives happened inside
        that car. When you closed the door
                and took off towards the urgency of your hearts.
Somewhere years ago in your life
        he's still waiting for you to pick him up and say *I'm sorry.*

## Truth Chamber

You're so huge when you're full of information
like your chest holds a larger heart.
To tell is to escape.
You want to hold so many things and without
is a word too lonely to define.
You want to be loved back like arms around your torso.
You know where to lead
like a soft echo you'll linger just a few moments behind
in a direction you believe in.
You're so handsome when you have something to say.
How many times should you have run, hands holding your ears,
retreating.
You're not an easy person, more of a scar.
You were scared to heal.
You wanted time to take us some kind of distance from today,
that's not on a map.
You can't choose what haunts you.
Even if you turn out the lights, close
your eyes, you can't disappear.
The dawn will bring light to your skin over and over
waking up every partaking part
illuminating the monsters you've mutated into.

You're so handsome when you have something to tell.
Under your influence how many times have you made others run?

## Glove Box

This is where
        you put pictures of people, not where they
                should be-
among manuals, maps, receipts-human records.
      In here you'll find
                photos of ghosts.
They're journals scribbled with notes
      of letters unread too long.
             You expected so much from the dead.

**Dial**

Your hands hover above the board
in the darkness of your bedroom you
play a game to contact the dead.
Others called this a word too difficult
to define-you called it reality.
If you find a lingering spirit as lonely,
your company is the favor.
You are told you were related in another life, the spirit you caught
shows in the movement of the dial.
Your wide eyes, your goose bumped skin,
neck-petrified-stiff,
hollowed out mouth reveals
just how much you are convinced.
Question after question takes you into another time, your previous lives
back to a bloodline that pulsed through you.
You're the one who lets go first,
too frightened, too fast.
You throw your hands up, off the dial, cover your mouth, your face, your eyes.
Your scalp begins to tingle; your chest is as if you've plunged, underwater, all your breath out of your lungs.
The spirit is furious, has stopped playing, stopped talking.
Your heart is a language so difficult to translate.
So ready to love anyone, you called upon the dead
to stay close, infinite.
You can't help your wicked pondering of that spirit speaking through games.

**Demon**

Tonight,
you're out reading the stars
trying to remember their stories

as if their meaning could articulate their shine.
This is about your shame,
The nakedness of humans,
There are so many you hunger for.

Their wholeness,
The heat of their skin,
The body's glow without a fabric cover.

You never mention your problem
with vodka, its swimming seduction.
Heating you up like sleeping in the sun.

You're afraid
of yourself, this lusting demon,
who aches to be used like a hotel room.

Downtown you find yourself going
where so many secrets are flickering in
blurry bedrooms.

You're consumed,
by this relentless urge to hunt
for someone,

a random lover to make you feel worth
his naked body.

You're grateful to be alive,
and always for the stars, their distraction,
their un-harmful company.

**Driver's Seat**

Inside here
    with the radio on.
        The music of your youth has found you.
Forsaken ballads where the singing sounds like weeping.
    These songs are for an afterlife.
        You're still taking breaths
among the living.
    You want to stop listening,
        though that would be like walking away from old friends.

## Doll

He liked you as his doll-
that outdated word for lovers.
Your hair is where he wanted his fingers to stay.
Can he teach you how to argue without words?
This must be a conversation
for your bodies, unclear androgynous language
he never let you close enough to learn.
He always questioned your importance,
like love had one ponderous paragraph printed
in a book left on a shelf for someone else's revelation.

## Weapon

He makes calls
to anyone.
*There's selfishness in all of us.*
*something no one can teach.*
He told you
while near a tender sleep
in a form of a whisper
barely words and then *You're a great friend.*
How will you know the way to escape those words?
If only you were clever enough to invent
a weapon for the heart.
A blanket full, thick, so warm
with transforming temperatures
where the moon repositions
and like creatures in stories
you become rampant
with your bodies.
Who was he calling in that mellow light?
He smelled like a night you knew would end too soon.
The dawn is magically unkind,
and your body will be nestled into the curve of his,
You'll contemplate your closeness, and its vanishing, his handsomeness
in the morning, in his slumber, and his humble unknowing.
Tomorrow these sweet hours will just be ordinary.
Your two warm bodies, beguiled, one unaware,
the other longing for a binding spell, an altering rebirth.

**Crystal**

The crystal orb hangs there
        from your rearview mirror
                this crystal for a necklace,
a bracelet, a charm.
        Though in here an orb
                that lures the sun
capturing the outside.
        How many faces have been lit by it?
Shards of rainbow
        on the floorboards
               and sparks of sequins
on the dashboard
        like in here
                it's a celebration.
Whoever takes a seat becomes a hologram.
        How long does someone stay real?
It hangs
        in the silver beetle
                like a telling stone
        provoking the mirages of the people you constantly crave.

**Omen**

Omen is a word you thought possessed magic-
like if you were to say it out loud a shift
would happen in your heart.
A word that casts shadows, so
unexpected, like when you ask a question
and you get a conversation that inquires facets of your faltering.
You're on the hunt where a certain word needs a story.
Where you prowl over what people say,
these little precious talks that tell you
just where your small life may be shining.

# Banner

*You described yourself as a banner wavering in the wind.*
        Your therapist reminds you of your word choice.

It's only been a week outside of her office your words are captured here
        their meaning lingering in this space
in waiting to be finished by your chaotic thoughts.

        *I've gathered you want to be seen, but not known.*
You don't say anything. To respond is to participate in the mystifying misunderstanding.

Where are all the windows? You think.
        This space with two faces staring at each other.
You want to interrupt because your therapist is wrong
        deceived by the wrongness of her notes-your skewed words.
*A white flag floating in the air.*
        You remember in certainty like your words were a tattoo
printed on an old lover who is somewhere in the map of your mind
        you're here to fix.
You don't say anything. You're here to listen.

**B**en **Westlie** holds an MFA in Poetry from Vermont College of Fine Arts. His work has appeared in the anthology *Time You Let Me In: 25 Poets Under 25* selected and edited by Naomi Shihab Nye, *Third Coast, The Fourth River, Atlas and Alice* and *The Battered Suitcase*. He is the author of three previous chapbooks *Sometimes Out of Turn, Extraordinary Construction* and *The Performance* all published by Finishing Line Press. His poetry had been featured on the radio station KAXE as an author on The Beat and has been a guest editor for *Split Rock Review*. Ben writes and works in St. Cloud, MN.

www.ingramcontent.com/pod-product-compliance
Lightning Source LLC
LaVergne TN
LVHW041525070426
835507LV00013B/1815